About the Book

Leading, understanding, and responding to change has been the biggest challenge for everyone. Selecting the best management framework and method is no different. To understand the project management framework's evolution. We must understand the history, needs, cause, and effect. This book is an attempt to provide some insights into agile frameworks.

This book will serve as a quick reference guide for agile concepts and frameworks. It has something for every reader; be it a novice or expert in agile.

Contents

About the Book
Preface – Vikas Brahmbhatt
Preface - Deepak Joshi
Agile Mindset
    Sports
    Rescue
Agility Alignment
Framework History
Rise of Framework
    Sequential Model:
    Incremental Approach:
    Lean process:
    Functional Agility:
    Team Agility:
    Timeboxing:
    Domain Frameworks:
    Life-cycle Frameworks:
Domain Framework
    Focus On Plan
        Plan-Do-Check-Act (PDCA)
        DMAIC
    Focus on Requirements
        Feature Driven Development (FDD)
        Rapid Application Development (RAD)
        Prototyping
    Focus on Design
        Model-Driven engineering Framework (MDF)
        Unified Modeling Language (UML)
    Focus on Code

- Clean code
- Extreme Programming (XP)
- Continuous Integration (CI)

Focus On Test
- Test-Driven Development (TDD)
- Behavior Driven Development (BDD)

Focus on Deployment
- DevOps

Agile Manifesto
- Values
- Principles of Agile

Lifecycle Frameworks
- DSDM
- Kanban
- Scrum
- LeSS
- Scrum Of Scrums
- SAFe
- DAD

Selection Of Framework

Activities in Agile

Preface – Vikas Brahmbhatt

I am a big fan of superheroes. It has been a constant struggle to find the best superhero. At first, I have tried to decide the best superpower. Speed, strength, invisibility, x-ray vision, firepower, teleportation, flying, etc. After many failed attempts, I have realized that the quality of superheroes should differentiate them. After many attempts, I have concluded one common factor in all superheroes. Irrespective of their superpower or enemy, they give first preference to saving civilians.

The second question, why do we need so many superheroes? With a variety of enemies, we needed a new kind of superhero to defend the world. The third question, how does the same enemy bring a new threat? As superheroes evolved, so does the challenge. Superheroes' had to use their power with a different approach to defeat the enemy.

I had the same questions for Agile project management.

Why do we need a new framework or method?

Why so many variations?

How to adopt it? Answers were the same.

As the agile project management framework evolved, the expectations and challenges increased. The team had to use their skills with a different approach.

Preface - Deepak Joshi

At the start of a regular day, fighter pilots assemble for a short briefing. The briefing includes a met-brief which includes possible wind speeds, directions, cloud levels, weather, and direction of runway to be used. This is followed by a quick session on emergencies and impediments. An emergency is simulated by one of the pilots. Right after the briefing, all pilots head out to see the flying plan and the time of the sorties. Each sortie has a purpose and flight plans well before the sortie.

The question arises, why pilots need a daily plan and why a lot of upfront details missing?

Do they know where enemy aircraft will approach? - No

Do they know what action the enemy aircraft will take? - No

That is why they have to be agile in their approach. They have to act as per the situation and there comes the idea of LRM (Last responsible moment).

Agile Mindset

Before we deep dive into the world of Agile. It is important to understand, what is the agile mindset? Adopting agile practices without an "Agile Mindset" will increase challenges, frustration, and chances of failure.

Mahatma Gandhi said

"Your beliefs become your thoughts,
Your thoughts become your words,
Your words become your actions,
Your actions become your habits,
Your habits become your values,
Your values become your destiny."

The team moving from traditional delivery to agile delivery approach must do the following.

Step 1: Empty Cup

Unlearn their existing practices, roles, and mindset.

Step 2: Learn

Learn what "Agile Mindset" is, understand agile framework and practices

Step 3: Apply

Apply their learning and embrace it

Step 4: Practice & Improve

Keep practicing, learn from your mistakes, and improve.

- Organizations are moving to an agile approach for reasons as following
- To stay with market trends
- To solve the problem faced during a traditional approach
- Better at responding to change
- High collaboration
- Higher velocity etc…

During this transition, many have missed the key ingredient i.e. "Agile Mindset".

For example, if we upgrade from "Petrol Car" to "Hybrid (Petrol + CNG) Car"; but still use it with petrol only. We will never gain benefits from a Hybrid car.

Like the above example if the organization adopts an agile delivery approach without an "Agile Mindset", they will never get desired benefits. Let us understand; what is the Agile Mindset? With some examples.

Sports

In every team sport, a player is selected for one primary skill and will strive towards giving his\her best in secondary skills. The primary goal in any sport is for the team to win.

For example, in "American Football," there are various roles, skills, and strategies. Irrespective of their role or skill during fumble the utmost priority for the player is to recover the ball. It is not a skill but the agility of players that makes this happen. The team who can recover the ball gets the opportunity of scoring. Similarly, if there is an opening or gap in the opposite team's defense; running towards the crossing line and gaining the yards is important. Again, irrespective of the primary skill of the player if they see an opening, they opt for it and that requires agility.

In the case of Cricket, fielding is a critical skill that is required from each player in a team. Normally to field or catch a single player is required, but lately, we have seen many instances that two fielders become one unit to stop the boundary. We have also seen instances where two-player work together to catch. These are the extreme agility examples that are not in any playbook.

In the case of Baseball; a fielder on the ground throws the ball to the fielder at the plate, but we have seen cases where a fielder on the ground has kicked the ball towards the fielder at the plate resulting in the runner getting out.

History depicts that teams written off by everyone have suddenly come out from a losing streak and became the champions due to an inspirational pep talk given by Coach or Player in the dressing room. Yes, that's right Pep Talks are not a skill in any game but might be the most important tool to boost the morale of any team.

Let's list down the kind of agility or agile mindset these teams have:

- Agility to React
- Agility to Response
- Collaboration
- Cross Function
- Communication and many more

Rescue

Teamwork is a major part of any successful rescue operation. The success of each task depends on someone else completing other related tasks with accuracy and within time.

In the case of Firefighting, the situation is assessed, and a rescue plan is created considering entry and exit point, fire control, the safety of people and property, containing the fire, and subsiding the fire. As per the plan, the workload is distributed, and duties are assigned. During the execution of the plan if the situation changes e.g. entry point is not safe or the exit strategy is not working. Instead of pushing the people to execute the plan; the plan is scrapped, reassessment and re-planning happen. As per the new plan, duties are redistributed and without any resistance, firefighters accept new duties and act on them.

During the rescue in the sea, the Scuba Diving team has to access multiple parameters before they start rescue operations like wind speed, wind direction, storm, sea tides, sea current, wreckage, probability of boat catching fire, etc... Unless they have a clear entry and exit strategy rescue does not start. It is to expedite rescue and ensure the safety of everyone.

SWAT team trying to rescue hostages has an entirely different approach and has very minimal response time on the ground during operation. If anyone gets injured another team member takes their position or shares the responsibilities. They show the highest level of collaboration even if they are on radio silence.

Let's list down the kind of agility or agile mindset these teams have:

1) Agility to increase the risk to avoid risk. For example, sending five firefighters to rescue two civilians from a burning building. I.e. increasing life risk by 250%

2) Agility to think on their feet. For example, changing the exit strategy during rescue

3) Agility to lead. For example, the next in command taking lead when the leader can't be reached or injured during a rescue operation.

4) Agility to accept failure. For example, Accepting the situation has changed and needs re-planning, keeping the ego aside.

As we have understood the agility mindset and how different kinds of agility might be required to achieve a goal. It will be important to understand how we can align the team and ensure they all are working in the same direction. The next chapter will talk about one such technique.

Agility Alignment

As Irish Novelist Maeve Binchy quotes

"Everyone is a hero in their own story if you look"

Every organization, team, and team member who has adopted agile practices tries to bring agility to the table. If the agility within a team is not aligned in the right direction it will become the biggest hurdle for the team's success.

"If our strengths are used in the wrong direction, they will become our biggest weakness"

In this chapter, we will understand the concept of agility alignment. You can call it a ritual, session, meeting, or as we like to call it a ceremony in an Agile world.

"AA (Agility Alignment)" ceremony is a must before starting any project that uses agile practices. Be it a novice, experienced, expert, or master team with Agile. As a team, we must lay down the expectation of the kind of agility is required to achieve the desired goal.

If you are already part of a team that is following agile practices and wondering if you need an agility alignment ceremony; the following will help you decide it.

During the start of a project if everyone in your team is excited and ready to run that extra mile. Now is any of the following true for your team?

- Team members have lost the zeal to outperform
- Team members becoming silent during team meets
- Is the team losing their cool and getting irritated?

- The product backlog is stagnant, even with the best effort from the team
- Decrease in velocity without any significant changes in requirement or team size?

If any of the above is true; you might need the "AA" ceremony more than you think. Before understanding agility alignment with examples, let us understand the why, what, and how for the "AA" Ceremony.

Why we need an "AA" ceremony?

Unlike the commonly accepted myth that says that agile promotes "What we can; we should deliver" the reality is agile promotes "What we must; we should deliver". To achieve this goal, the team must spend their energy in the same direction. The "AA" ceremony provides the required platform for the team to understand deviations within the team's mindset and do course correction when required.

What is the outcome of the "AA" ceremony?

The team will agree to a common goal. The team will list down the kind of agility required to achieve that goal.

When should we have the "AA" ceremony?

At the start of a project. After each goal is achieved. If requested by any team member. If a goal has changed.

Who should attend and contribute to the "AA" ceremony?

Everyone in your agile team.

Who should moderate the "AA" ceremony?

Scrum Master

How many goals can be agreed on in the "AA" ceremony?

Maximum one

Let us understand it from an example. As shown in the diagram; we have assembled a team, and everyone has an agile mindset. But without the "AA (Agility Alignment)" ceremony; everyone is trying to bring agility for what they think is best. In this approach, only two potential outputs can be achieved: slow progress or product failure.

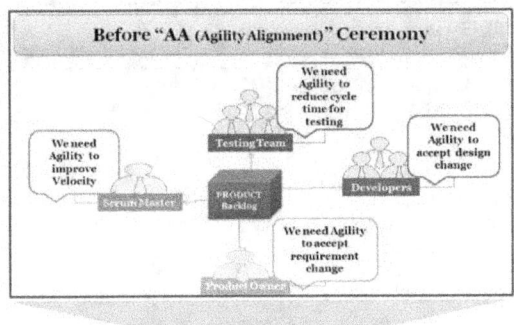

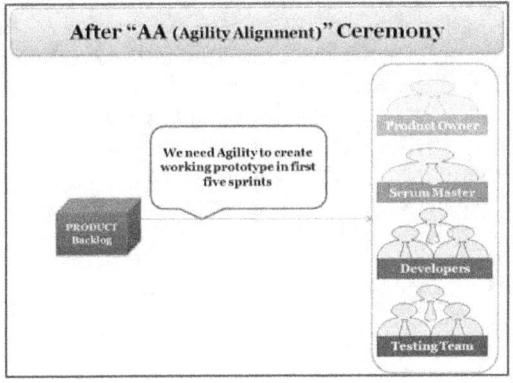

As we can see the "AA" ceremony is run with a clear goal in mind and the team must understand, accept and align their approach to achieve their goal. During the ceremony, a detailed discussion is required to agree on the kind of agility required to achieve that goal.

Following are a few examples of the "Agility Alignment" ceremony.

The goal is to improve velocity by 20 percent in the next three sprints

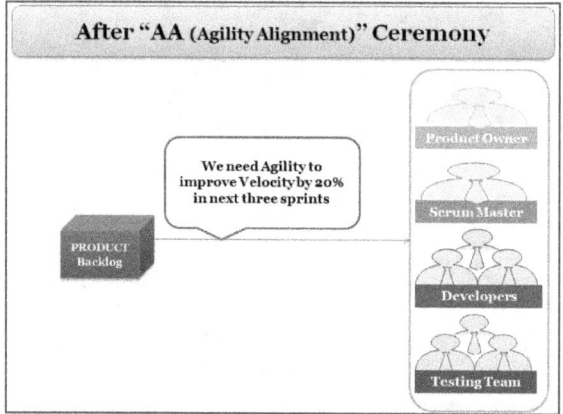

In this example to improve velocity; the team might agree to a re-prioritize backlog, reduce test cycle, faster deployment to QA, product owner provides more time to clarify the team's questions.

The goal is to complete the top three features in the next four sprints.

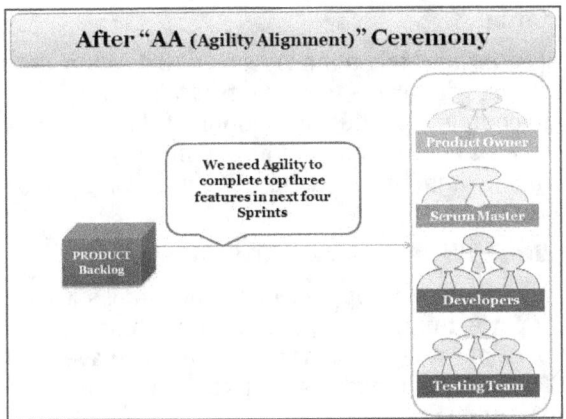

In this example, to complete the top three features team might accept responsibility to groom user stories with required details, a tester might accept helping complete design input documents, a developer might extend the unit testing scope to cover additional test scenarios reducing cycle time to complete quality assurance.

As Farshad Asl quotes

"Be fast, be first, but never be alone. Nothing can replace the value of teamwork"

The idea is for a team to align their effort towards achieving the same goal.

As we have understood what agility alignment is and how we can utilize this technique. Let us understand why it is crucial for newly formed teams.

As Tuckman's model suggests each newly formed team goes through four key phases.

- Forming
- Storming
- Norming

- Performing

Let us assume a project team is formed to develop a project which will need ~100 sprints (10 days in each sprint) to complete product development. Let us see both scenarios and understand how agility alignment can help improve the efficiency of the team.

Scenario 1) Without an agility alignment

In this case, the team might cross the norming stage and start performing after spending approximately 30% to 40% of project time as shown in the image below. That will be between sprint 30 to 40 as shown in the diagram below.

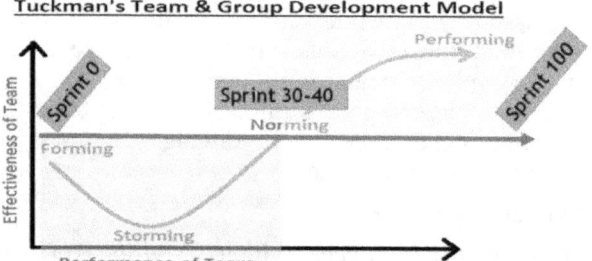

Scenario 2) With agility alignment

In this case, the team will be going through all four stages during each agility alignment goal. Resulting in the identification of problem areas earlier in the life cycle. As shown in the diagram team will be crossing the norming stage and start performing after the 3rd or 4th agility alignment ceremonies as shown in the image below. That will be between spring 15 to 20, assuming AA 1 to 4 are of 5 sprints each.

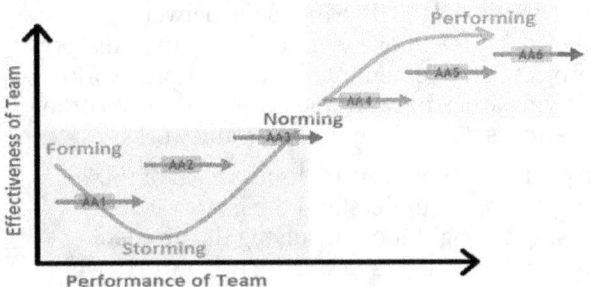

Framework History

Before we do a deep dive into agile delivery frameworks; it will be essential to know the history of project management methods and frameworks. Following are a few examples, there are many other frameworks derived from given frameworks.

The prime reason for us to discuss each of these frameworks and understand the history is that choosing the right tool for solving the problem always helps. Insights into these frameworks will help you choose the best fit for your needs.

For Example, will you use a single tool for all following scenarios or different tools?

- Spread butter on bread
- Cut a tree
- Cut bread loaf into slices
- Smash boiled potatoes

The correct answer is different tools. Like the above example, don't choose the framework because the industry opted for it or competitor is using it. Choose it according to your needs to solve the given problem.

1930: Plan-Do-Check-Act (PDCA)

PDCA is an iterative four-step management method is used in project management. Many project management frameworks evolved before IT became Industry and PDCA is one of them.

1940: Lean

Lean is a systematic method of reducing waste without compromising on productivity.

1980: Iterative & Incremental Development (IID)

IID is a method used for Iterative Design and Incremental Build.

1980: Rapid Application Development (RAD)

RAD is an adaptive software development approach. It follows prototype instead of design specifications.

1980: Model-Driven Engineering (MDE)

MDE focuses on creating a conceptual representation of system relationships. Simplifying process of design over detailed specifications.

1984: Theory Of Constraints (TOC)

TOC focuses on finding constraints and restricting connected processes around the system. It adopts the principle "Chain is no stronger than weakest link".

1990: Team Software Process (TSP)

TSP helps team managers to organize projects and building teams by identifying goals, roles, and related work. It supports methods to measure and derive metrics to improve the software process.

1992: Crystal

Crystal is about developing software by focusing on people, interactions, skills, talents, communication, and community. It is a people-centric framework and prescribes a wider range of roles.

1993: Microsoft Software Framework (MSF)

MSF is a set of principles, models, methods, concepts, and guidelines for delivering information technology services. It is the first comprehensive framework covering the complete development lifecycle. Including project management practices, CMMI, Agile, and risks methods and processes.

1993: Refactoring

Refactoring focuses on identifying long and duplicate codes. It advocates rewriting the code to remove duplicate code without impacting functionality. Provides the benefits of maintainability and extensibility. To be more agile in product support and enhancements.

1994: Dynamic System Development Methods (DSDM)

DSDM covers a complete development life cycle adopting iterative and incremental models with a foundation on the RAD process. It includes management practices for the project life cycle by following lean methods.

1995: Scrum

Scrum is a lightweight framework based on iterative and incremental models. It introduced the concept of "Timebox" called sprints. Promotes forming small teams (3-9 members). It recommends defining roles and follow a simple method to manage teams. We will discuss this framework in detail in the following chapter.

1995: Pair Programming

It recommends two programmers working together to write better quality code. Eliminating waste in form of defects and preventing re-work. Thus, enabling agile and lean ways.

1996: Personal Software Process (PSP)

PSP is a structured software development process that helps software engineers better understand and improve their performance by bringing discipline to the way they develop software.

1997: Feature Driven Development (FDD)

FDD is an agile framework. As its name suggests it organize software development around making progress on features.

1999: Adaptive Software Development (ASD)

ASD is a direct outgrowth of an earlier agile framework, Rapid Application Development. It embodies the principle that continuous adaptation of the process to the work at hand is the normal state of affairs.

1999: Extreme Programming (XP)

XP is a code-first approach to software delivery that emphasizes four basic activities. Coding, Testing, Listening, and Designing.

1999: Unified Process (UP)

UP is an iterative and incremental software development process framework.

1999: Continuous Integration (CI)

CI is the process of taking features from the program backlog and developing, testing, integrating, and validating them in a staging environment where they are ready for deployment and release.

2001: Agile Manifesto

The Agile Manifesto is a proclamation that articulates 4 key values and 12 principles that its authors believe software developers should use to guide their work.

2002: Test-Driven Development (TDD)

TDD is a software development process that relies on the repetition of a very short development cycle.

First, the developers write an (initially failing) test case, then produce the minimum amount of code to pass the test. Finally, refractors the new code to acceptable standards.

2003: Lean Software Development (LSD)

LSD is a translation of lean manufacturing principles and practices to software development.

2005: Large Scale Scrum (LeSS)

LeSS is a framework for scaling agile and scaling Scrum. It decreases organizational complexity.

2006: Behavior Driven Development (BDD)

BDD is a software engineering process that stems from TDD (Test Driven Development) and ATDD (Acceptance Test Driven Development).

2007: Scrum Of Scrum (SOS)

SOS is a scaled agile technique for integrating the work of multiple Scrum teams (usually five to nine members each) working on the same project.

2007: Software Kanban (SK)

SK is a method of managing the creation of products with an emphasis on continual delivery. It also ensures not to overburden the development team.

2008: Clean Code (CC)

CC is a list of guidelines and examples that can help developers improve their programming quality and write better, cleaner code.

2009: DevOps

DevOps is a set of software development practices that combines software development (Dev) and information technology operations (Ops) to shorten the system development life cycle; while delivering features, fixes, and updates frequently in close alignment with business objectives.

2011: Scaled Agile Framework (SAFe)

SAFe is a set of organization and workflow patterns intended to guide enterprises in scaling lean and agile practices.

2012: Disciplined Agile Delivery (DAD)

DAD is a people-first, learning-oriented hybrid agile approach to IT solution delivery. It has a risk-value delivery lifecycle, is goal-driven, is enterprise aware, and is scalable.

2015: Nexus

It is a framework that drives to the heart of scaling by minimizing cross-team dependencies and integration issues.

Rise of Framework

Why these frameworks were developed? What problems these frameworks have been trying to address? What practices and principles this framework recommends?

During the early stage of software development, the team focused on business automation. They helped users to provide services much quicker and cut operating expenses by introducing computers in their business process. During this time automation of a process by the computer itself was a huge win.

Sequential Model:

The development team came up with a sequential process representing development phases. This model was a waterfall. The sequential process enabled the team to build and deliver better software. Only a few players in the market developed and released products for customers.

Incremental Approach:

Years later, many players entered the development market resulting in more competition. At the same time, industries were struggling to manage finances and were required to cut expenses. The demand for software products to deliver at less cost and quicker was in great demand. A new process was soon identified to build software products in an incremental approach. This process was the IID - Iterative and incremental development process. It prevented customer rejections and increased adoptions.

Lean process:
As market dynamics became more competitive, companies required better and improved methods. They had to improve performance and reduce wastage to run at profits. It was essential to reduce market time and accept changes to stay ahead of the competition. Throughput processes and methods helped to meet these demands. These new processes and methods were called lean processes. It became popular and its adoption increased in the corporate.

Functional Agility:
The lean influenced all professionals across industries and gave rise to new frameworks. Each framework brought agility to respective practices in industries. Product development became much easier and quicker. They also avoided common conflicts and confusion within teams.

Team Agility:
After improving functional agility, team agility gave birth to agile team processes. The new agile team process resulted in the rise of life cycle frameworks to improve team agility. These frameworks extended domain or functional frameworks for better team results.

Timeboxing:
Soon, the timeboxing of development resulted in the Scrum. Timeboxing (iteration with fixed length) reduced lead and cycle time. It insisted that the team focus on customer interactions and business values.

More regular reviews and retrospectives resulted in quality delivery with satisfied customers.

Over time evaluation of different frameworks took two separate routes.

Domain Frameworks:
One set of frameworks tried to resolve on the ground micro-level problems. Focused on single-phase, domain, or industry practice. We can classify them as "Domain Framework".

Life-cycle Frameworks:
The second set of frameworks tried to address macro-level problems. Focused on the entire life cycle of software development. We can classify them as "Life-cycle Frameworks".

The following chapters will talk in-depth about domain and life-cycle frameworks.

Domain Framework

As software development became mature, lean processes were being adopted in Industry. Soon sequential, iterative, or incremental models were not enough for development teams. Problems faced by the team were more complex than before.

- Customer priorities shared with the sales team did not reach the development team in time
- Rework and changes resulted in a longer delivery time
- Business needs were changing faster than product delivery, resulting in failed products
- Need to reduce ambiguity in requirements and avoid rework was high
- Information loss during handover caused chaos and confusion
- Creating, updating, and tracking plans were impossible due to frequent changes
- Delay in approval of plan resulted in delayed delivery

The industry still had a "Sequential Mindset". The first set of frameworks focused on planning problems. The success of these frameworks triggered the offspring of many domain frameworks. Each domain framework focused on one phase of the development life-cycle.

Focus On Plan

Plan-Do-Check-Act (PDCA)

The Plan-Do-Check-Act cycle is a model for carrying out change. It is an essential part of the lean manufacturing philosophy and a key prerequisite for continuous improvement of people and processes.

It is used for a new product or concept development, problem-solving, project implementation, and many other fields.

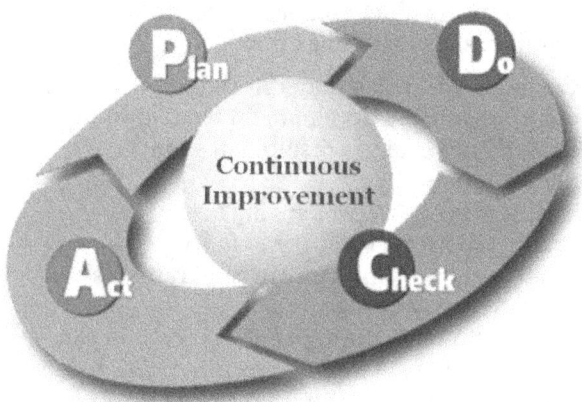

DMAIC

DMAIC refers to a data-driven quality strategy for improving processes and is an integral part of the company's Six Sigma Quality Initiative. DMAIC is an acronym for five interconnected phases: Define, Measure, Analyze, Improve, and Control.

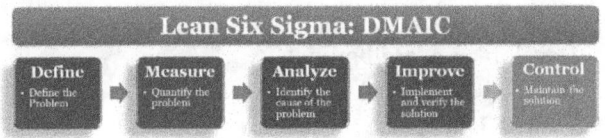

Focus on Requirements

Feature Driven Development (FDD)

Feature Driven Development was designed to follow a five-step development process, built largely around discrete "feature" projects based on user interactions.

- Develop an overall model
- Build a features list
- Plan by feature
- Design by feature
- Build by feature

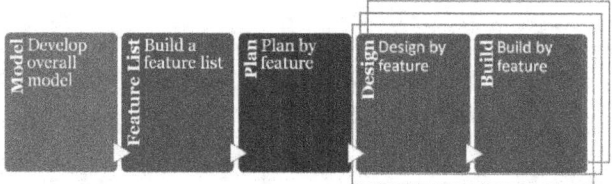

Rapid Application Development (RAD)
The Rapid Application Development model is a type of incremental model. In the RAD model, the components or functions are developed in parallel as if they were mini projects. The developments are time-boxed, delivered, and then assembled into a working prototype.

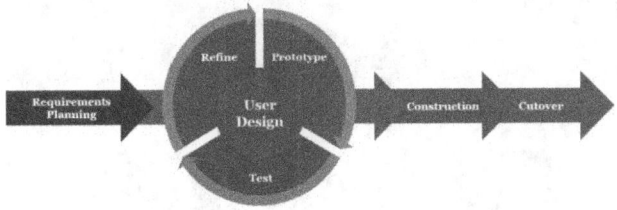

Prototyping

The prototyping model is a systems development method. A prototype (an early approximation of a final system or product) is built, tested, and then reworked as necessary until an acceptable prototype is finally achieved from which the complete system or product can now be developed.

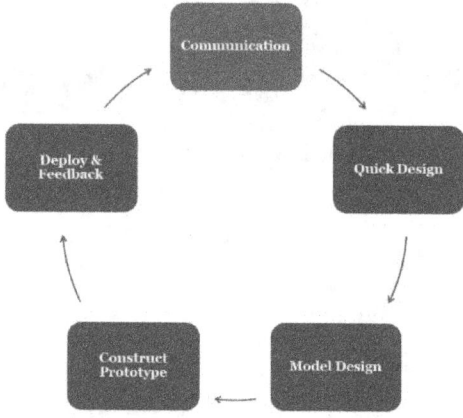

Focus on Design

Model-Driven engineering Framework (MDF)

As the strategic value of software increases for many companies, the industry looks for techniques to automate the production of software and to improve quality and reduce cost and time-to-market. These techniques include component technology, visual programming, patterns, and frameworks. Businesses also seek techniques to manage the complexity of systems as they increase in scope and scale. They recognize the need to solve recurring architectural problems, such as physical distribution, concurrency, replication, security, load balancing, and fault tolerance.

Unified Modeling Language (UML)

Unified Modeling Language, is a standardized modeling language consisting of an integrated set of diagrams, developed to help system and software developers for specifying, visualizing, constructing, and documenting the artifacts of software systems, as well as for business modeling and other non-software systems.

The UML represents a collection of best engineering practices that have proven successful in the modeling of large and complex systems. The UML is a very important part of developing object-oriented software and the software development process. The UML uses mostly graphical notations to express the design of software projects. Using the UML helps project teams communicate, explore potential designs, and validate the architectural design of the software.

Focus on Code

Clean code

Clean code is focused on best practices in the industry to provide maximum benefits towards readability, reusability, extendibility and, maintainability.

- It should be elegant—Clean code should be pleasing to read. Reading it should make you smile the way a well-crafted music box or well-designed car would.
- Clean code is focused —Each function, each class, each module exposes a single-minded attitude that remains entirely undistracted, and unpolluted, by the surrounding details.
- Clean code is taken care of. Someone has taken the time to keep it simple and orderly. They have paid appropriate attention to details. They have cared.
- Runs all the tests
- Contains no duplication
- Minimize the number of entities such as classes, methods, functions, and the like.

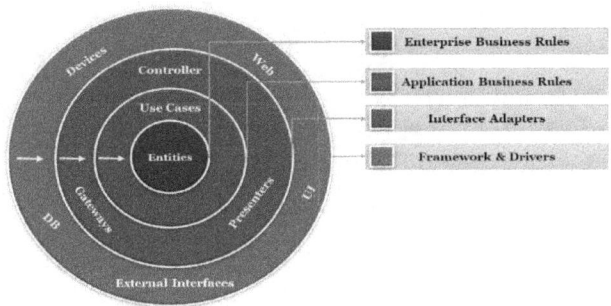

Extreme Programming (XP)

Extreme Programming (XP) is an agile software development framework that aims to produce higher quality software and a higher quality of life for the development team. XP is the most specific of the agile frameworks regarding appropriate engineering practices for software development.

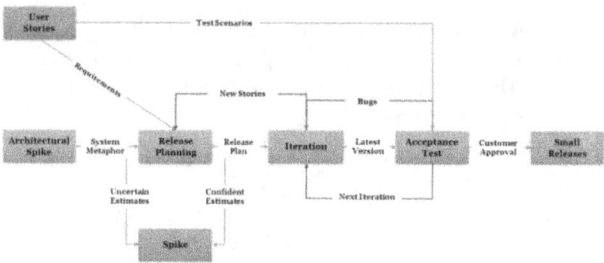

The five values of XP:

- Communication
- Simplicity
- Feedback
- Courage
- Respect

Continuous Integration (CI)

Continuous Integration (CI) is a development practice that requires developers to integrate code into a shared repository several times a day. Each check-in is then verified by an automated build, allowing teams to detect problems early.

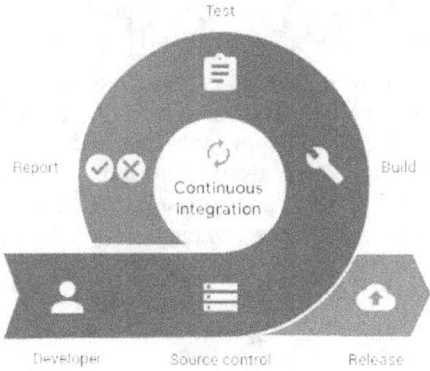

Continuous integration principles:
- Maintain a code repository
- Automate the build
- Make the build self-testing
- Everyone commits to the baseline every day
- Every commit (to baseline) should be built
- Keep the build fast
- Test in a clone of the production environment
- Make it easy to get the latest deliverables
- Everyone can see the results of the latest build
- Automate deployment

Focus On Test

Test-Driven Development (TDD)

Test-Driven Development can be defined as a programming practice that instructs developers to write new code only if an automated test has failed. This avoids duplication of code. TDD means "Test Driven Development". the primary goal of TDD is to make the code clearer, simple, and bug-free.

Test-Driven Development starts with designing and developing tests for every small functionality of an application. In a TDD approach, first, the test is developed which specifies and validates what the code will do. The process is more common with developers and is adopted as part of the coding phase rather than in the testing phase.

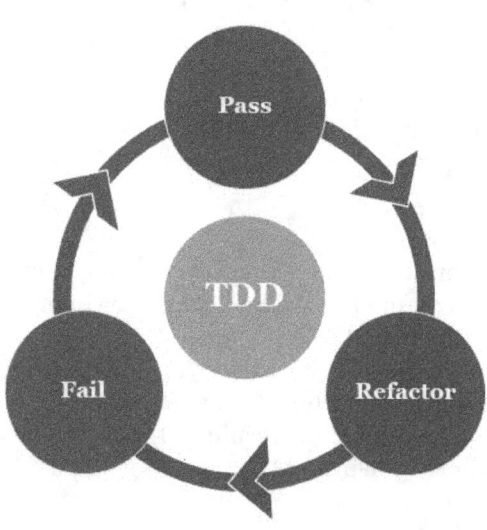

Two levels of TDD

- **Acceptance TDD (ATDD):** With ATDD you write a single acceptance test. This test fulfills the requirement of the specification or satisfies the behavior of the system. After that write just enough production/functionality code to fulfill that acceptance test. The acceptance test focuses on the overall behavior of the system. ATDD also was known as Behavioral Driven Development (BDD).
- **Developer TDD:** With Developer TDD you write a single developer test i.e. unit test and then just enough production code to fulfill that test. The unit test focuses on every small functionality of the system. Developer TDD is simply called TDD.

The main goal of ATDD and TDD is to specify detailed, executable requirements for your solution on a just-in-time (JIT) basis. JIT means considering only those requirements that are needed in the system. To increase efficiency.

Behavior Driven Development (BDD)

Behavior Driven testing is an extension of TDD. Like in TDD in BDD also write tests first and then adds application code. The major difference that we get to see here are

- Tests are written in plain descriptive English type grammar
- Tests are explained as a behavior of an application and are more user-focused
- Using examples to clarify requirements

This difference brings in the need to have a language that can define, in an understandable format.

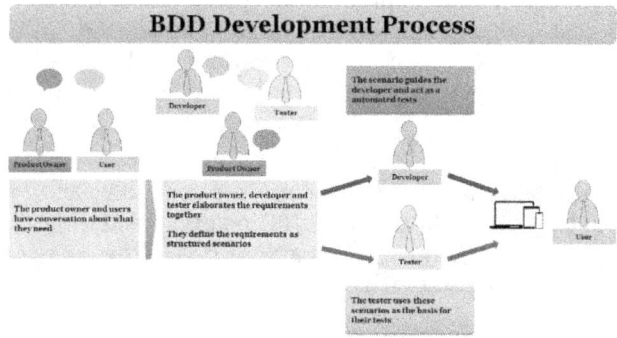

Features of BDD
- Shifting from thinking in "tests" to thinking in "behavior"
- Collaboration between Business stakeholders, Business Analysts, QA Team, and developers
- Ubiquitous language, it is easy to describe
- Driven by Business Value
- Extends Test-Driven Development (TDD) by utilizing natural language that non-technical stakeholders can understand

Focus on Deployment

DevOps

DevOps is the blending of development and operations. It is meant to represent a collaborative or shared approach to the tasks performed by a company's application development and IT operations teams.

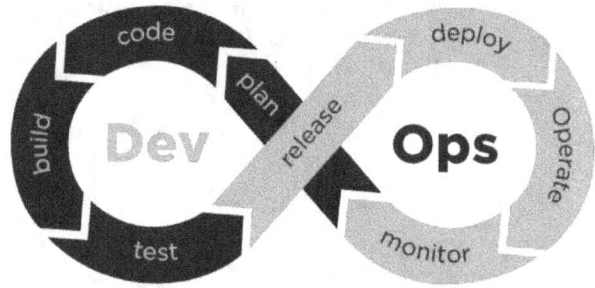

The term DevOps is used in several ways.

Broad interpretation: DevOps is an operational philosophy that promotes better communication between these teams.

Narrow interpretation: DevOps describes the adoption of automation and programmable software development and infrastructure deployment and maintenance.

Agile Manifesto

February 2001. Seventeen individuals representing Extreme Programming, SCRUM, DSDM, Adaptive Software Development, Crystal, Feature-Driven Development, Pragmatic Programming, and others gathered to find common grounds. What emerged was the Agile "Software Development" manifesto.

The seventeen signatories to the manifesto proclaimed that they value.

- **Individuals and interactions** over processes and tools
- **Working software** over comprehensive documentation
- **Customer collaboration** over contract negotiation
- **Responding to change** over following a plan

The manifesto for Agile Software Development is based on twelve principles

1. Customer satisfaction by early and continuous delivery of valuable software
2. Welcome changing requirements, even in late development
3. Deliver working software frequently (weeks rather than months)
4. Close, daily cooperation between businesspeople and developers
5. Projects are built around motivated individuals, who should be trusted
6. A face-to-face conversation is the best form of communication
7. Working software is the primary measure of progress

8. Sustainable development, able to maintain a constant pace
9. Continuous attention to technical excellence and good design
10. Simplicity—the art of maximizing the amount of work not done—is essential
11. Best architectures, requirements, and designs emerge from self-organizing teams
12. Regularly, the team reflects on how to become more effective and adjusts accordingly

The Agile movement is not anti-methodology, in fact many of us want to restore credibility to the word methodology. We want to restore a balance. We embrace modeling, but not in order to file some diagram in a dusty corporate repository. We embrace documentation, but not hundreds of pages of never-maintained and rarely-used tomes. We plan, but recognize the limits of planning in a turbulent environment. Those who would brand proponents of XP or SCRUM or any of the other Agile Methodologies as "hackers" are ignorant of both the methodologies and the original definition of the term hacker.

— Jim Highsmith

Values

1. Individuals and interactions over processes and tools

Value people and communication over process and tools as it makes it more responsive. Once people are aligned and they understand the needs, they will use processes and tools to expedite delivery or resolve problems. It also allows individuals to bring to the table what they can offer to deliver the desired output.

2. Working software over comprehensive documentation

Traditional software development practices had many documentation deliverables tied with each phase. Over time many of these documents became hurdles instead of value addition. Agile does not eliminate documentation. It takes an approach "Do Minimum To Get Maximum". It focuses on the bottom line, minimum or streamlined documents to enable the development team for producing the required deliverables.

3. Customer collaboration over contract negotiation

Traditionally customers were involved in negotiating the contracts defining details on required deliverables. The team negotiating the contract and the team delivering the products were different teams in large projects. Information flow was normally one way. Collaboration enables customers to be part of the development team and provides a two-fold advantage.

4. Responding to change over following a plan

Traditionally change was seen as a hindrance in the plan. A significant amount of effort was being spent to anticipate, avoid or accept the change. The collaborative approach enabled the team to embrace the change instead of avoiding it.

Principles of Agile

Customer satisfaction through early and continuous software delivery.
Reduction in wait time, early delivery, and frequent releases resulted in increased customer satisfaction.

Accommodate changing requirements throughout the development process.
The collaborative nature of delivery reduced the delay caused during information handover and eliminated the ambiguity. The team embraced the change and aligned the effort to accommodate the needs of the business.

Frequent delivery of working software.
Timeboxing and continuous delivery enabled the frequent release of working software.

Collaboration between the business stakeholders and developers throughout the project.
Two-way information exchange empowered the team to take a real-time decision toward supporting requirements or design changes.

Support, trust and motivate people involved.
Empowering and enabling people resulted in innovative, quality-driven, higher velocity delivery.

Enable face-to-face interactions.
Communication is more successful when development teams are co-located.

Working software is a primary measure of progress.
Working towards the "Bottom-Line".

Agile process to support a consistent development pace.
Repeatable and maintainable approach for delivering working software.

Attention to technical design and design enhances agility.
Focus on the right design to enable the team for a repeatable and maintainable approach. A feedback mechanism enables the team to improve after every release.

Simplicity.
Focus on right now to accomplish the required deliverables.

Self-organizing team encourages great architectures, requirements, and designs.
Skilled and empowered teams take ownership, make decisions, and collaborate to produce quality products.

Regular reflection on how to become more effective.
Retrospective enables the team to provide feedback for required changes in process, design, approach, or skills.

Lifecycle Frameworks

As the focus shifted to find better frameworks to manage end-to-end software development. The first to roll out based on new lean processes and practices were DSDM, MSF, and UP.

The DSDM focused on prototyping and best practices of the RAD process and methods. It promoted flexibility and clarity in software construction methods. It also embraced lean practices for cost-effective development. It had challenges since prototyping did not help in all contexts. It turned out to be more of a burden to a few teams and non-acceptance was getting increased. They prefer to adopt traditional models like a waterfall for less complex scenarios.

Yet, since it did not improve team agility, the experts looked out for better frameworks. They required speed and quality without compromising on scope, time, and cost. The Kanban board was becoming very popular. TQM (Total Quality Management) and TPM (Total Productivity Management) adoptions challenged experts.

It took time to roll out the team process complementing the lean process. A new team process with a time limit for life cycle phases got proposed. This new process soon became popular as Scrum. It enabled more frequent interaction, retrospectives, and reviews with customers and stakeholders.

The above process became popular and got adopted by the technical team. The Scrum framework focused on the team and became a better life cycle model. Timeboxing, retrospective, and short standups complemented better team interaction and bonding. Promoting ownership, self-organizing, and collaboration resulted in quicker delivery and boost innovation.

The Scrum became the de facto life cycle framework for the team. It further evolved to support large teams. Frameworks like LeSS, Scrum of Scrum, SAFe, and DAD rolled out supporting large team sizes.

Lack of agile organizational team process resulted in frameworks like SAFe and DAD. The new frameworks enabled external teams like pre-sales, sales, support, and operations. They even embraced other agile frameworks to benefit the organization and corporate teams.

DAD team embraced more on IID, Unified Process, RAD, Scrum, and other lean processes. DAD accommodated matrix roles against agile artifacts. Here, the team owns artifacts like backlogs made up of epics, features, and stories.

SAFe embraced value-chains, XP, dev-ops, and Kanban. The artifacts got mapped against portfolios, programs, and projects. It mandates at the level of the artifact and enforces agile practices at the organization level.

In this chapter, we will discuss each of these lifecycle frameworks. We will discuss key aspects and the basics of these frameworks. Once you have identified a framework for your use; a detailed study specific to the framework of your choice will be required.

DSDM

Dynamic System Development Method (DSDM) is an agile project delivery framework. Early release of DSDM sought to provide discipline to the RAD method. DSDM was later revised to provide a generic approach to project management and solution delivery.

DSDM provides a four-phase framework:
- Feasibility and business study
- Functional model / prototype iteration
- Design and build iteration
- Implementation

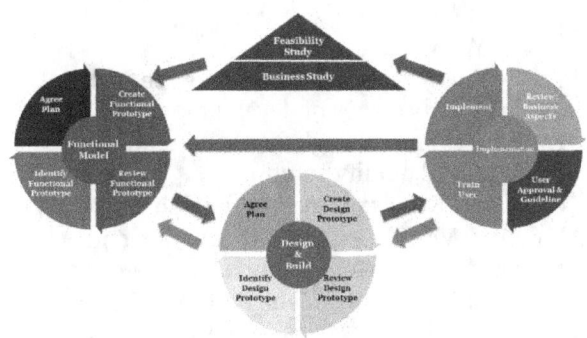

The eight Principles of DSDM:
- Focus on the business need
- Deliver on time
- Collaborate
- Never compromise quality
- Build incrementally from firm foundations
- Develop iteratively

- Communicate continuously and clearly
- Demonstrate control

DSDM is vendor-independent, covers the entire life-cycle of a project. DSDM provides best practice guidance for on-time, on-budget delivery of projects. It has the proven scalability to address projects of all sizes and for any business sector.

DSDM advocates the use of several proven practices, including:

- Timeboxing: Incremental delivery approach by breaking down the project into portions
- MoSCoW Prioritization categories:
    - Must have
    - Should have
    - Could have
    - Won't have
- Prototyping: Creation of the prototype of the system at early stages of development
- Testing: Testing throughout each iteration to ensure a good quality solution
- Workshop: Brings project stakeholders together
- Modeling: Visualize a business domain and diagrammatic representation of the system
- Configuration Management: At the end of each time-box, the deliverables from various streams need to be well managed

DSDM is designed to be easily tailored and used in conjunction with traditional methods. DSDM complements methods such as PRINCE2® or other agile approaches such as Scrum.

Kanban

Kanban is a visual system for managing work as it moves through a process. Kanban visualizes both the process (the workflow) and the actual work passing through that process. The goal of Kanban is to identify potential bottlenecks in your process and fix them so work can flow through them cost-effectively at optimal speed or throughput.

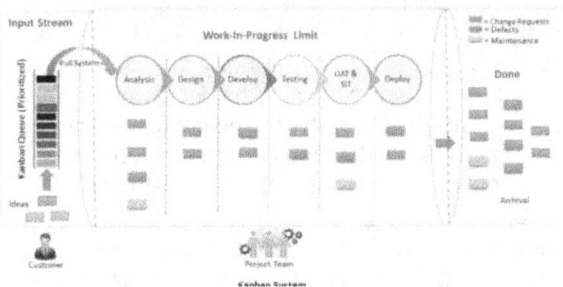

A Kanban system ideally controls the entire value chain from the supplier to the end consumer. In this way, it helps avoid supply disruption and overstocking of goods at various stages of the manufacturing process. Kanban requires continuous monitoring of the process. Particular attention needs to be given to avoid bottlenecks that could slow down the production process. The aim is to achieve higher throughput with lower delivery lead times. Over time, Kanban has become an efficient way in a variety of production systems.

The Kanban Method follows a set of principles and practices for managing and improving the flow of work. It is an evolutionary, non-disruptive method. Kanban promotes gradual improvements to an organization's processes. If you follow these principles and practices, you will be able to use Kanban for maximizing the benefits to your business process. This will help improve flow, reduce cycle time, increase value to the customer. These all are crucial to any business today.

The four foundational principles and six Core Practices of the Kanban Methodology are provided below:

Foundational Principles

- Start with what you are doing now: The Kanban Method emphasizes not making any change to your existing setup/ process right away. Kanban must be applied directly to the current workflow. Any changes needed can occur gradually over some time at a pace the team is comfortable with.
- Agree to pursue incremental, evolutionary change: Kanban encourages you to make small incremental changes. It suggests to avoid making radical changes that might lead to resistance within the team and organization.
- Respect current roles, responsibilities, and job titles: Unlike other methods, Kanban does not impose any organizational changes by itself. So, it is not necessary to make changes to your existing roles and functions which may be performing well. The team will collaboratively identify and implement any changes needed. These principles help the organizations overcome the emotional resistance and the fear of change.
- Encourage acts of leadership at all levels: Kanban encourages continuous improvement at all levels of the organization. and it says that leadership acts don't have to

originate from senior managers only. People at all levels can provide ideas and show leadership to implement changes. This will continually improve the way they deliver their products and services.

Core practices of the Kanban method

- Visualize the flow of work: This is the fundamental first step to adopting and implementing the Kanban method. You need to visualize the process steps that you currently use to deliver your work or your services. Depending on the complexity of your process and your work mix, your Kanban board can be very simple to very elaborate. Once you visualize your process, then you can visualize the current work that you and your team are doing.
- Limit WIP (Work in Progress): Limiting work-in-progress is fundamental to implementing Kanban – a 'Pull-system'. By limiting WIP, you encourage your team to complete work at hand first before taking up new work. Thus, work currently in progress must be completed and marked done. This creates capacity in the system, so new work can be pulled in by the team.
- Manage flow: Managing and improving flow is the crux of your Kanban system after you have implemented the first 2 practices. A Kanban system helps you manage flow by highlighting the various stages of the workflow and the status of work in each stage. Depending on how well the workflow is defined and WIP Limits are set, you will observe either a smooth flow of work piling up as something gets held up. All this affects how quickly work traverses from start to the end of the workflow (some people call it

value stream). Kanban helps your team analyze the system and make adjustments to improve flow to reduce the time it takes to complete each piece of work.
- Make process policies explicit: As part of visualizing the process, it makes sense to also define and visualize policies. Create a common basis for all participants to understand how to do any type of work in the system. The policies can be at the board level, at a swim lane level, and for each column. They can be a checklist of steps to be done for each work item type. Entry-exit criteria for each column, or anything at all that helps team members manage the flow of work on the board well.
- Implement feedback loops: Feedback loops are an integral part of any good system. The Kanban method encourages and helps implement feedback loops. Review stages in Kanban board workflow, metrics, and reports provide continuous feedback on work progress – or the lack of it – in the system.
- Improve collaboratively, evolve experimentally: The Kanban method is an evolutionary improvement process. It helps you adopt small changes and improve gradually at a pace and size that your team can handle easily. It encourages the use of the scientific method – forms a hypothesis, tests it, and makes changes depending on the outcome of the test. The key task of a team implementing Lean/ Agile principles is to evaluate the process constantly and improve continuously.

The concept of "Flow"

At the core of Kanban is the concept of "Flow". This means that the cards should flow through the system as evenly as possible, without long waiting times or blockages. Everything that hinders the flow should be critically examined. Kanban has different techniques, metrics, and models. If these are consistently applied, can lead to a culture of continuous improvement (kaizen).

The concept of Flow is critical. Measuring and improving flow metrics can dramatically improve the speed of delivery processes. This also improves the quality of products or services by getting faster feedback from customers.

Scrum

Scrum is a framework that helps teams work together. Scrum encourages teams to learn through experiences, self-organize while working on a problem, and continuously improve.

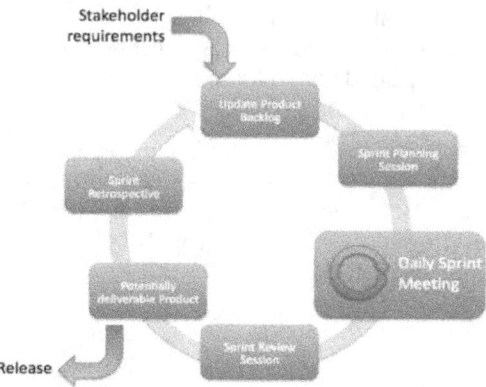

Its principles can be applied to all kinds of teamwork. This is one of the reasons Scrum is so popular.

SCRUM is not an acronym. It was named after rugby's Scrum. Scrum is a light framework with only a few key rules and a limited set of practices.

Benefits of Scrum:

- Risk mitigation due to faster feedback cycles
- Reduced time-to-market hence improved ROI (return on investment)
- Improved stakeholders satisfaction
- Confidence to succeed in a complex product development

The Scrum team consists of three roles:

- Product owner: The most empowered central point of product leadership
- Scrum master: Acts as a coach, providing process leadership, helping the Scrum team. Scrum master also helps the organization develop its organization-specific Scrum approach
- Development team: A cross-function team that handles designing, building, and testing the desired product

Scrum has three artifacts:

- Product backlog
- Sprint backlog
- Potentially shippable product

Activities:

- Sprint planning
- Daily Scrum
- Sprint review
- Sprint retrospective

One of the important activity which is commonly practiced in Scrum is product backlog grooming.

LeSS

LeSS is a scaled-up version of one-team Scrum, and it maintains many of the practices and ideas of one-team Scrum. In LeSS, you will find:

- a single product backlog (because it's for a product, not a team)
- one definition of done for all teams
- one potentially shippable product increment at the end of each sprint
- one product owner
- many complete, cross-functional teams (with no single-specialist teams)
- one sprint

In LeSS all teams are in a common sprint to deliver a common shippable product, every sprint.

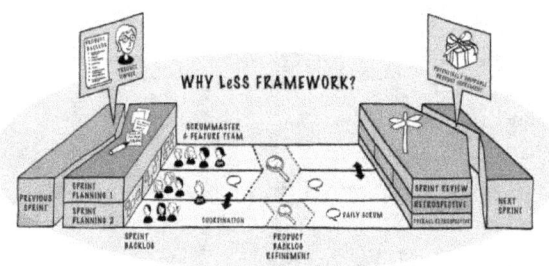

What's different in LeSS?

- Sprint planning part 1: In addition to the one Product Owner, it includes people from all teams. Let team members self-manage to decide their division of Product Backlog Items. Team members also discuss opportunities to find shared work and cooperate, especially for related items.

- Sprint Planning Part 2: This is held independently (and usually in parallel) by each Team, though sometimes for simple coordination and learning two or more Teams may hold it in the same room (in different areas).
- Daily Scrum: This is also held independently by each Team, though a member of Team A may observe Team B's Daily Scrum, to increase information sharing.
- Coordination: Just Talk, Communicate in Code, Travelers, Open Space, and Communities.
- Overall PBR: There may be an optional and short overall Product Backlog Refinement (PBR) meeting that includes the one Product Owner and people from all teams. The key purpose is to decide which teams are likely to implement which items and therefore select those items for later in-depth single-team PBR. It is also a chance to increase alignment with the Product Owner and all teams.
- Product Backlog Refinement: The only requirement in LeSS is single-team PBR, the same as in one-team Scrum. But a common and useful variation is multi-team PBR, where two or more teams are in the same room together, to increase learning and coordination.
- Sprint Review: In addition to the one Product Owner, it includes people from all teams, and relevant customers/users, and other stakeholders. For the phase of inspecting the product increment and new items, consider a "bazaar" or "science fair" style: a large room with multiple areas, each staffed by team members, where the items developed by teams are shown and discussed.

- Overall Retrospective: This is a new meeting not found in one-team Scrum, and its purpose is to explore improving the overall system, rather than focusing on one Team. The maximum duration is 45 minutes per week of Sprint. It includes the Product Owner, Scrum Masters, and rotating representatives from each Team.

Scrum Of Scrums

Scrum of Scrums Framework – Managing multiple Scrum teams by representation for the same product or project.

The Scrum of Scrums is a scaling mechanism. Scrum scales fractally and by doing so limits the number of communication pathways needed to transmit information relevant to the success of the enterprise. The Scrum of Scrums is analogous to the team level daily Scrum except for the Scrum of Scrums. It is a virtual team composed of representatives from individual Scrum teams that collaborate to integrate and shape a product(s). The Scrum Masters and anyone else needed to deliver the Scrum of Scrums collaborative Definition of Done meet and communicate impediments, progress, and any cross-team coordination that needs to happen by answering for the team the same three questions used in the Daily Scrum.

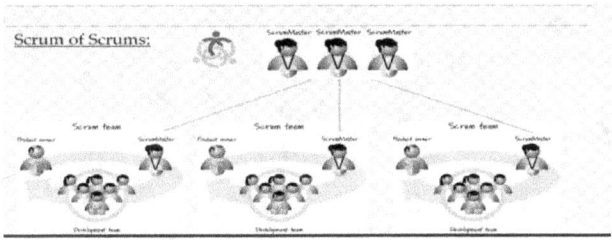

A technique to scale Scrum up to large groups (over a dozen people), consisting of dividing the groups into Agile teams of 5-10. Each daily Scrum within a sub-team ends by designating one member as "ambassador" to participate in a daily meeting with ambassadors from other teams, called the Scrum of Scrums.

SAFe

SAFe is designed to help businesses efficiently deliver value on a regular and predictable schedule.

It provides a knowledge base of proven principles and practices to support enterprise agility.

It provides a simple, lightweight experience for the software development team. The whole framework is divided into three segments Team, Program, and Portfolio. There is one optional segment- Large Solution.

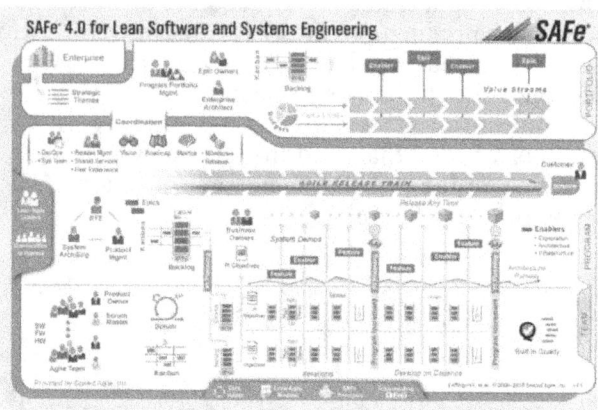

SAFe allows team for,

- Implementing Lean-Agile software and systems at enterprise-level
- It's based on Lean and Agile principles
- It gives detailed guidance for work at the enterprise Portfolio, Value Stream, Program, and Team
- It's designed to meet the needs of all stakeholders within an organization

Let's see how the Scaled Agile framework is different from other agile practices,

- It's publicly available and free to use
- Available in a highly approachable and usable form
- It's lightweight, practically proven results, and specific to level
- It constantly/regularly modifies/maintains the most commonly used agile practices
- Offers useful extensions to common agile practices
- Grounds agile practices to an enterprise context
- Offers a complete picture of software development
- Visibility or transparency is more on all levels
- Continues or regular feedback on quality and improvement

Scaled Agile Framework (SAFe): It stands on the foundations of its

- Lean-Agile Principles
- Agile Core Values
- Lean-Agile Leadership
- Lean-Agile Mindset

1) SAFe Lean-Agile Principles

These basic principles and values for SAFe must be understood to get the desired results.

- Take an economic view
- Apply systems thinking
- Assume variability; preserve options

- Build incrementally with fast, integrated learning cycles
- Base milestones on an objective evaluation of working systems
- Visualize and limit WIP, reduce batch sizes and manage queue lengths
- Apply cadence, synchronize with cross-domain planning
- Unlock the intrinsic motivation of knowledge workers
- Decentralize decision-making

2) SAFe Agile Core Values

The SAFe agile is based on these four values.

Alignment:

SAFe supports alignment. Alignment starts at, strategic themes in portfolio backlog and moves down to vision and roadmap of program backlogs and then moves to the team's backlogs.

Built-in Quality:

It ensures that every incremental delivery reflects the quality standards. Quality is not "added later" is built-in. Built-in quality is a prerequisite of Lean and its mandatory

Transparency:

Transparency is the enabler for trust. SAFe helps the enterprise to achieve transparency at all levels. Everyone can see into the portfolio backlog/kanban, program backlogs/kanban, and team backlog/kanban. Each level has a clear understanding of the PI goals. Agile release trains have visibility into the team's backlogs, as well other program backlogs. Teams and programs have visibility into business and architecture Epics. They can see what might be headed their way.

Program Execution:

SAFe places great focus on working systems and resultant business outcomes. SAFe is not useful if teams can't execute and continuously deliver value.

3) Lean-Agile Leaders:

The Lean-Agile Leaders are lifelong learners and teachers. It helps teams to build better systems through understanding and exhibiting the Lean-Agile SAFe Principles. As an enabler for the teams, the ultimate responsibility is adoption, success, and ongoing improvement of Lean-Agile developments. For change and continuous improvement, leaders must be trained. Leaders need to adopt a new style of leadership. One that truly empowers and engages individuals and teams to reach their highest potential.

Principles of these Lean-Agile Leaders

- Lead the change
- Know the way; emphasize lifelong learning
- Develop people
- Inspire and align with the mission
- Minimize constraints
- Decentralize decision making
- Unlock the intrinsic motivation of knowledge workers

4) Lean-Agile Mind-Set:

Lean-Agile mindset is represented in two things:

- The SAFe House of Lean

- Agile Manifesto

The SAFe House of Lean:

SAFe is derived from Lean manufacturing principles and practices. Based on these factors SAFe presents the "SAFe House of Lean". It is inspired by the "house" of lean Toyota. The goal of lean is unbeatable, to deliver maximum customer value in the shortest lead time with the highest possible quality to the customer.

DAD

Disciplined Agile Delivery (DAD) is a people-first, hybrid agile approach to IT solution delivery. It has a risk-value delivery lifecycle, is goal-driven, is enterprise aware, and is scalable.

DAD promotes a full delivery lifecycle and defines three explicit phases. These phases are Inception, Construction, Transition.

- Inception: Where you initiate the project
- Construction: Where you build/configure the solution
- Transition: Where you deploy the solution into production or the marketplace

DAD explicitly addresses the full delivery lifecycle, instead of just the construction portion of it. The vast majority of agile teams need to do some explicit upfront work to get going, a fair bit of construction work, and some work to deploy.

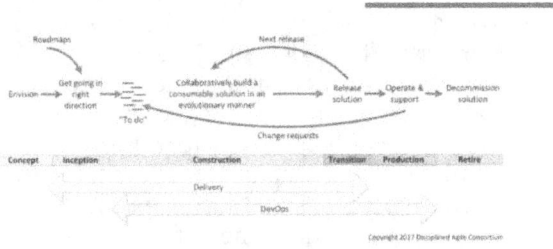

DAD picks up where Scrum leaves off. DAD describes how all agile techniques fit together, going far beyond Scrum, to define a full agile solution delivery lifecycle. Like Scrum, the DAD addresses leadership, roles & responsibilities, and requirements change management. Unlike Scrum DAD doesn't stop there, it also addresses other important aspects of software development such as architecture, design, testing, programming, documentation, deployment, and many more. In short, DAD provides a much broader understanding of how agile development works in practice, doing a lot of the "heavy process lifting" that Scrum leaves up to you.

- DAD is pragmatic. The DA toolkit provides choices, not prescriptions, enabling you to easily tailor a strategy that reflects the situation that your team finds itself in. To do this effectively you need to understand the process-oriented choices you have and what the trade-offs are. DAD makes these choices explicit through its process-goal-driven approach.
- DAD supports both lean and agile ways of working (WoW). DAD supports several delivery lifecycles, including a Scrum-based agile lifecycle, a Kanban-based lean lifecycle, two continuous delivery lifecycles, a Lean Startup-based exploratory lifecycle, and a Program "team of teams" lifecycle. Teams find themselves in unique situations, and as a result, one process size does not fit all. Even in small companies, we've seen situations where some teams are taking an agile approach, some a lean approach, and some combinations thereof.
- DAD is based on empiricism. For several years Scott Ambler, Mark Lines, and many other contributors to DAD worked in or visited hundreds of enterprises around the world in a wide range of industries and environments. DAD, and the DA toolkit in general, captures the proven strategies

adopted by these organizations, describing the strengths and weaknesses of each strategy and providing guidance for when and when not to apply them.
- DAD provides a solid foundation from which to scale agile. DAD supports the successful scaling of agile and lean techniques in several ways. First, its full delivery lifecycles and breadth of software development advice answer how to successfully apply agile in practice. Second, its goal-driven approach provides the required flexibility for tailoring your agile process to meet the challenges faced by agile teams working at scale. Third, DAD builds in many foundational concepts required at scale, including DevOps, explicit agile governance, and enterprise awareness.
- DAD enables and goes beyond SAFe. SAFe leaves the details of construction to you and as a result, can prove to be fragile in many organizations. DAD provides the solid process foundation missing from SAFe and is complementary to SAFe. DAD describes several strategies for organizing large or geographically distributed teams. It describes a range of options for scaling your approach to agile and lean software development, giving you context-sensitive options that SAFe doesn't.
- DAD teams deliver solutions, not just software. DAD recognizes that the software we develop runs on hardware, which may need upgrades, and is supported by documentation. Our stakeholders may also

need to evolve their business processes, and sometimes even their organizational structures, to address the new needs of the situation that they face. In short, DAD teams deliver solutions that comprise software, hardware changes, supporting documentation, improved business processes, and even organizational changes.
- DAD is evolving. We're constantly learning as practitioners, learning about and experimenting with new agile and lean strategies all of the time. These learnings are constantly being applied to evolve DAD.

There are several ways that DAD differs from Scrum:

- Greater lifecycle breadth. DAD supports a full delivery lifecycle, going beyond Scrum's construction lifecycle to also provide advice for how to effectively initiate an agile project (or product) and how to transition/release into production. In other words, it helps take some of the mystery out of how all this agile stuff works in practice.
- Focus on enterprise awareness. A strength of Scrum is its inward focus within a project team to minimize distractions and thus enabling the team to focus on delivering on its commitments to their stakeholders. Focus is achieved using concepts such as the Product Owner, collocation, whole team, and daily Scrums. However, this inward focus and self-reliance can lead to silo behavior whereby the team ignores enterprise concerns such as basic governance, reuse of assets, patterns, templates, and guidelines. Disparate architectures and systems that are difficult to maintain can result. DAD

encourages teams to be enterprise aware, and to include the Architecture Owner role, to ensure that good enterprise practices are not ignored and that collaboration occurs between projects and enterprise authorities as required.
- Greater practice breadth. DAD is a hybrid decision process framework that adopts strategies from a wide range of sources, including Scrum, Extreme Programming (XP), Agile Modeling, Kanban, Outside In Development (OID), and many more and shows how they fit together. Instead of focusing on a small part of the overall delivery process, as Scrum does, DAD addresses a much wider scope and as a result, provides more robust and effective guidance to agile teams.
- Less prescription. DAD promotes a goals-driven approach that enables more effective tailoring and scaling. For example, one of the DAD process goals is to address changing stakeholder needs. Where Scrum prescribes a single way to do this, the product backlog, DAD gives you several options (Product backlog, Work item list, Work item pool, Formal change management) as well as advice for when to consider each strategy. DAD also defaults to the Work item list, a more robust extension of a Product backlog, giving you a good starting point. Another goal is to coordinate activities. Where Scrum prescribes a 15-minute daily meeting called a Daily Scrum Meeting or Daily Stand Up, DAD gives you several options to choose from and walks you through how to choose the right approach for you.
- Less branding. One of the philosophies we took when describing DAD was that we wanted to

move away from the process branding that we've seen occurring in the agile
community. Although DAD is flexible when it comes to terminology, for example, if you want to use the term Sprint instead of Iteration then go right ahead, DAD defaults to non-branded terms. So for example we use the terms Coordination Meeting over Scrum Meeting, Team Lead over ScrumMaster, Retrospective over Sprint Retrospective, and so on.

Selection Of Framework

The selection of the Agile Framework depends on the situation, cultural landscape, and appetite for change. It is important to choose the right mix of Agile practices. It is also very important to understand why our team or our organization is considering using an Agile approach.

- What issues are we facing that our traditional approach is felt ineffective?
- Why do we believe that an Agile approach will help us to achieve our goals?

Once we get the answers to the above two points, the following will be helpful to identify the right framework.

Framework	Team size	Roles
Kanban	Not defined	Not defined. Few teams practice Kanban with the Scrum roles.
Scrum	<9 members	Product Owner, Scrum Master, Development team
Scrum of Scrums	>9 up to 5 Scrum teams	Each team will have the same roles as in Scrum team. **Additional:** Chief Product Owner, Scrum of Scrums Master **Executive Action Team** (A

		team consisting of top-level executives. Chief Product Owner is part of this team.) **Executive Meta Scrum Team** (The Meta Scrum is how the Product Owner (PO) role scales in Scrum. The Meta Scrum is a virtual team made up of four to five Product Owners that coordinate Epics, product releases, and product lines)
DAD (Disciplined Agile Deliveries)	Small Agile Teams- 2 to 15 members Medium Sized Teams- 12 to 50 members Large Teams/Programs- >35 members [With each kind/size of the team, the team structure changes]	**Primary roles:** Product Owner, Team leader, Architecture Owner, other required team members **Supporting roles (temporary):** Domain expert, Technical Expert, Independent tester, Expert (as per need), Integrator
SAFe	Team Level- 5 to 9 members	Each team will have the same roles as in the

	Program level- 5-12 teams	Scrum team including any specialist required. **Additional:** Program level- Release Train Engineer (Chief Scrum Master), System Architect, Product Management (PM), DevOps, Business Owners, User Experience Designers
LeSS	One team- Same as Scrum LeSS Huge- >8 Scrum teams	Feature team(s): Development team with Scrum Master. Product Owner (Team) Head of the Product Group

Activities in Agile

The following table will help you understand key activities that will be required for any agile framework or methodology

Backlog Planning	**User-story:** Identifies and creates all user stories for the workable or final product. **Feature/Theme:** Related user-stories are grouped based on functionality domain are called Feature **Epic/Goal:** The goal of product or purpose of the product is stated in Epic Note: All information and details required for functionality or user-story might not be available during backlog work items creation.
Backlog Refinement	Refinement is a review process focused on identifying priority and ensuring required information and details along with **acceptance criteria** are available for the team. Note: All information and details may not be available for the complete backlog list, however, ensure high priority items are well defined before sprint can start.
Backlog Grooming	Grooming is important communication and collaboration process to brief or walkthrough

		work-items or functionalities to the team to ensure clarity.
	Backlog Estimates	Once grooming is done, Estimation kick-offs. The team determines the complexity of each functionality and identifies tasks to perform with the effort required to complete with available information.
	Sprint Planning	Once estimated. Sprints are planned to complete the product. Number of sprints is derived either by velocity or by capacity against story points or effort. After a number of sprints are determined, the backlog items are allocated to each sprint based on the order of priority.
	Sprint Board	Represents work items movement from one stage to another in table format.
	Sprint review	Sprint review focuses and ensures work items or user stories have enough details and acceptance criteria to be worked upon in sprint towards completion. Any customer changes on completed functionalities or user-story may be added by moving scoped one to the next sprint. At the sprint review stage, it is required all details must present with acceptance criteria. The team

	can either accept or reject work-item based on can complete or cannot. Sprint review revisits a number of additional sprints required to complete backlog items. It's important to the product owner and Scrum master to determine on financial impact and get acceptance from a customer or descope work items from the backlog.
Scrum meeting or stand-up meeting	A short meeting to know the impediments of a team.
Showcase	The showcase is an opportunity to show off the great work, the team has been doing and get feedback from the product owner or end customer.
Sprint Retrospective	It helps the team to connect and communicate on things that can be improved to upcoming sprint objectives and overall product goals. It also helps in deciding key strategies and approaches to be adopted based on the project or product environment.
Velocity measurement	It is a crucial metric that determines team ability to deliver work items and impact towards product delivery schedule.

Burndown	The work completed and remaining against allocated in graphical format.

About Author – Vikas Brahmbhatt

Vikas Brahmbhatt has been in the IT industry for over seventeen years. He has extensive work experience in both the service and product industries. He has completed a Bachelor of Engineering in Computers. He has worked with major IT giants like TCS, Accenture, Teradata, ATOS, Capgemini, Polaris, Rolta, Civica to name a few. He has worked across various industry segments for example Retail, Leas & Loan, Insurance, Banking, Media & Entertainment, Government sectors. Over the years he has been recognized to improve team's productivity via streamlining the processes, use of innovation, and mentoring the team to improve productivity by reducing waste. His core experience lies in business intelligence and analytics and he has been known for helping teams to excel by adopt agile practices within traditional delivery frameworks.

About Author – Deepak Joshi

Deepak Joshi has been in the IT industry for over fourteen years. He is a Certified Scrum Master, Certified Scrum Product Owner, and Certified Scrum Professional. His educational background includes a Masters in Computer Science and a Masters in Economics. He also served twenty years' service in defence. This has given him a broad base from which to approach many topics. Deepak helps teams to understand and adopt agile practices during software development. By following the agile way of working, he helps the teams to adopt an agile mindset. He believes in transparency, openness, collaboration. In his view, the 'pull' way of working yields the required results than having a push work environment. He believes in Being agile than Doing agile. He enjoys facilitating various games during sprints. He also invented a few games and tried those in various teams. Teams got very positive and intended results out of these games. Deepak believes to work in collaboration with stakeholders. At times, he explains to them the benefits of the agile model of project deliveries. For the last many years, he is a proponent of Agility.

www.ingramcontent.com/pod-product-compliance
Lightning Source LLC
Chambersburg PA
CBHW070445220526
45466CB00004B/1770